treasures
of the
transformed
life

PARTICIPANT'S WORKBOOK
and
LEADER'S GUIDE WITH DVD

treasures
of the
transformed
life

satisfying your soul's thirst for more

PARTICIPANT'S WORKBOOK
and
LEADER'S GUIDE WITH DVD

Based on the book by John Ed Mathison

contents

acknowledgments and credits

This Participant's Workbook is based on the forty-day study book, Treasures of the Transformed Life: Satisfying Your Soul's Thirst for More by John Ed Mathison, pastor of Frazer Memorial United Methodist Church in Montgomery, Alabama, without whose support, wisdom, and direction this project would not have happened.

Thank you, John Ed, and your wonderful staff at Frazer, in particular, the Frazer Television Ministry staff of John Rogers, director; Courtney Johnson; and Lauren Webster.

The art used for this resource and in its corresponding components is copyright Steve Cohen/FoodPix/Jupiterimages. Original art direction, cover design, and page design were by Joey McNair, Providence Publishing Corporation. The editorial development group included Fiona Soltes, writer; Abingdon Press staff; and the Providence Publishing Corporation team of Andrew B. Miller, publisher; Melissa Istre; Mark Jacobs; Holly Jones; Joey McNair; Tammy Spurlock; and Nancy Wise.

introduction

Do you ever just listen to the rain? It can be such a powerful thing to witness showers from heaven pour down on dry ground.

Sometimes, a rainstorm will come up quickly. Everything's bright and blue; but before you know it, you're standing there, drenched. Other times, though, it starts with a drop here and a drip there, and the pitter-patter slowly grows to a steady soak.

Our relationship with God can be the same way. Sometimes, when we least expect it, there he is—coming through for us in a mighty fashion. But at other times, we might need to look more closely to see his raindrops, his constant presence around us that grows as we become more aware of it.

The material you hold in your hands can help you learn to recognize that rain. It can also help you enjoy the soaking that only comes in his presence and the satisfaction that stems only from a life transformed.

Through a series of questions, discussions, Scripture readings, and a willingness to dive deeper into the depths that God has for you, the coming weeks could very well change your perspective and quench your thirst in all areas of your life.

In order for that to happen, you're going to have to step out in faith. Your level of commitment and participation will have a lot to do with the outcome. So what will the coming rain mean to you?

study format

This *Participant's Workbook* is meant to be used in conjunction with the book *Treasures of the Transformed Life: Satisfying Your Soul's Thirst for More* by John Ed Mathison. That text is grouped into six parts, with forty days' worth of personal readings and introspective questions. Each day of *Treasures of the Transformed Life* ends with questions that, it is hoped, you will answer with much prayer, taking the time to really think them through and asking God for his revelation and guidance.

If you'd like to take notes on what you discover along the way, you'll find journal pages at the beginning of each part in this workbook. These Insights sections are to help you reflect on what you read and on what God is revealing to you through this forty-day study. They're for your private observations; what you write won't be shared with your small group.

This *Participant's Workbook* is designed to be the compass for making sure we get everything out of each week's study that we possibly can. Keep it handy while you read the daily book chapters, bring the workbook with you when you attend your weekly small group session, and expect God to move as he ties it all together.

Here's how the next six weeks will unfold. We'll begin each small group gathering with a short DVD message from John Ed Mathison. Then, we'll go over the main points of that week's chapter using a fill-in-the-blank format, and perhaps initiate some preliminary discussion.

We'll then divide into smaller groups or pairs to give you the opportunity to share on a more personal level. At the close of each meeting, we'll look at Scripture that will help guide you in the coming week.

During our six-week study, you'll notice that other activities in the church body will tie into the weekly subjects as well. That's because we're all in this together. No matter where we are in our walk with God, there's always more to learn, share, and receive.

part I

priming
the pump

insight & application

Insight—use the space on these pages to record your personal reflections, any thoughts, observations, or revelations that you discover in reading *Treasures of the Transformed Life*.

Application—after recording your insight, consider how you might make positive changes in your life or way of thinking in response to what you have read.

This discipline will assist you in remembering and possibly sharing with your group or class some of the reflections that have come to you during this forty-day journey.

1: The need for more

insight _____

_____

_____

_____

_____

_____

application _____

_____

_____

_____

_____

2: God really does care

insight _____

_____

_____

_____

_____

application _____

_____

_____

_____

_____

3: Great expectations

insight _____

_____
_____
_____
_____
_____

application _____

_____
_____
_____
_____

4: Finding a niche

insight _____

_____
_____
_____
_____

application _____

_____
_____
_____
_____

5: Love your neighbor

insight _____

_____

_____

_____

_____

_____

application _____

_____

_____

_____

_____

6: Overcoming obstacles

insight _____

_____

_____

_____

_____

application _____

_____

_____

_____

_____

7: Time to commit

insight _____

_____

_____

_____

_____

application _____

_____

_____

_____

_____

_____

small group

introduction

Hello and welcome! Let's begin with prayer that God will bless this time together (*prayer*). Now let's dive into *Treasures of the Transformed Life* by reading this workbook's introduction and study format aloud. Your small group or Sunday school leader will look to one of you to volunteer to do the reading.

Now it's time to watch a brief DVD message by John Ed Mathison, author of *Treasures of the Transformed Life: Satisfying Your Soul's Thirst for More.*

post-dvd discussion

Let's open up discussion with the following questions and statements. First, let's read each question and fill in the blank. Then we'll dive deeper into each concept. Would someone care to read the first one aloud?

1. Psychologists tell us that most people in America today are

   _____.

   If we listen to popular culture, what are the things that are supposed to satisfy us? Do they?
2. Great pain in life comes when we're _____.

   How does God make himself available to us to help fill that void?
3. The one who made you, God himself, is absolutely _____ to you.

   How could a true revelation of God's love for you change the way you live your life?
4. God expects a commitment from us that is _____ and not one that looks good on the outside.

   What does it mean to have an authentic relationship with God?

5. If we decide to live our lives only according to what we want, we run the very real risk of missing God's _____.

   What could be the benefits of discovering and fulfilling God's plan for our lives?

6. God doesn't just call us into a relationship with him; he also wants us to be in relationship with other _____.

   Why is it so important to be part of the bigger picture of the church family?

personal application

Now divide into smaller groups or pairs to discuss questions posed by this week's readings and topic. The first items are the main points for discussion. It's important that everyone has the opportunity to participate and respond to these. If you cover the first group of questions quickly, you may want to delve deeper by considering some of the supplemental questions.

key discussion questions

- At this point in your life, for what are you thirsty?
- Are you willing to get a little more wet (to go deeper into what God wants of you)? What would it take for you to respond yes to that question?

supplemental questions

- What do you need to take to God that you previously thought was too small for him to be bothered with?
- What would it take for you to give God more of your time, your thoughts, yourself?
- Is there someone (an individual or a group) you need to love, regardless of how you feel about them?

looking ahead

During the coming week, we'll read about prayer. Let's hide this Scripture verse in our hearts (see Psalm 119:11) to help us remember what's most important:

> I am the vine; you are the branches. Those who remain in me, and I in them, will produce much fruit.
>
> —John 15:5

part II

drawing
water

8: Tapping into the source

insight _____

_____

_____

_____

_____

application _____

_____

_____

_____

_____

9: Prayer defined

insight _____

_____

_____

_____

_____

application _____

_____

_____

_____

_____

10: Line of communication

insight _____

_____

_____

_____

_____

application _____

_____

_____

_____

_____

11: Scenario for prayer

insight _____

_____

_____

_____

_____

application _____

_____

_____

_____

_____

12: Standing in the gap

insight _____

_____

_____

_____

_____

application _____

_____

_____

_____

13: Products of prayer

insight _____

_____

_____

_____

_____

application _____

_____

_____

_____

14: Praying with power

insight _____

_____

_____

_____

_____

application _____

_____

_____

_____

_____

_____

small group

introduction

Let's pray *(prayer)*.

We began our study with an introduction to the idea that God loves us, he's committed to us, and he expects us to be committed to him in return.

This past week, we've focused on prayer. Have you memorized the Scripture that talks about the importance of remaining plugged in? Write it below, and then we'll say it together.

_____

_____

_____

_____

_____

Let's watch a DVD message from John Ed Mathison, followed by a few discussion questions.

post-dvd discussion

Let's consider the following questions and statements. As we did last week, we'll fill in the blanks, then dive deeper into each concept.

1. We all go through times when it seems like God is _____ or that our prayers aren't being heard.
   How can God use ebb and flow in our prayer lives to encourage us to pursue him?

2. David tells us that people who are blessed—the ones who delight in the Lord—are like _____ planted along the riverbank.

   How is a committed, faithful Christian like a firmly planted tree?

3. Prayer is simply a _____ with God.

   Why are people intimidated by prayer?

4. Prayer is not _____; if you pray for something, it's not just automatically going to happen.

   Why would God not answer a prayer?

5. Prayer is not just a list of things we want, it is actually a means to _____ with God in his work.

   How can an active prayer life allow God to work through us?

6. The Bible calls prayer for others "_____ in the _____."

   Why is it important for us to pray for others, as well as ourselves?

personal application

Now divide into smaller groups or pairs to discuss questions posed by this week's readings and topic. If you cover the key questions quickly, consider some of the supplemental questions.

key discussion questions

- When was a specific time you saw God answer a prayer? How did that make you feel? How did those involved react?
- Have you seen God's hand move in response to your prayers this week?

supplemental questions

- What is God waiting for you to collaborate with him to do?
- Where does your will need to bend to God's?
- Where does God want you to commit to stand in the gap for others through prayer?

looking ahead

During the coming week, we'll read about presence. Let's memorize this Scripture verse to help us remember what's most important:

Since we are all one body in Christ, we belong to each other, and each of us needs all the others.

—Romans 12:5

jumping in
with both feet

15: Pulling together

insight _____

_____

_____

_____

_____

application _____

_____

_____

_____

_____

16: God our father

insight _____

_____

_____

_____

_____

application _____

_____

_____

_____

_____

17: Brothers and sisters in Christ

insight _____

_____

_____

_____

_____

application _____

_____

_____

_____

_____

18: Family gatherings

insight _____

_____

_____

_____

application _____

_____

_____

_____

_____

19: Where priorities lie

insight _____
_____
_____
_____
_____

application _____
_____
_____
_____
_____

20: Do your part

insight _____
_____
_____
_____
_____
_____
_____
_____

21: Commit to community

insight _____

_____

_____

_____

_____

application _____

_____

_____

_____

_____

small group

introduction

Let's pray *(prayer)*.

We're now bringing our third week of *Treasures of the Transformed Life* to a close. Our previous focus had been on prayer and the importance of staying connected to God so we can partner with him in his work. This past week, we concentrated on presence. Have you memorized the Scripture? Write it below and then we'll say it together.

_____

_____

_____

_____

_____

Let's watch this week's DVD message from John Ed Mathison.

post-dvd discussion

Let's open up some discussion by filling in the blanks. Then we'll dive deeper into each concept.

1. God calls us to be part of his _____.

    As the Father of the church family, how might God be different from a father here on earth?

2. In addition to learning to relate to one another, love each other, forgive each other, and care for each other, being part of God's family means we _____ each other.

    Why is it important for Christians to look out for one another?

3. God also calls us to _____, or bring others under his umbrella of love.

     What does it mean to "make disciples of all the nations?"

4. Just as with any family, we feel _____ when we don't regularly come together.

     What kind of advantages could there be to knowing and being known in a church family?

5. One of the top reasons people give for not going to church is that they're just too _____.

     What does the story of Mary and Martha teach us about being full of activity?

6. God's family should be a picture of _____, with each person participating.

     What are some of the ways church members can show grace and mercy to each other?

personal application

Divide into smaller groups to discuss the questions raised by this week's concepts. Remember, everyone should have the opportunity to participate. If you get through the key questions quickly, move on to the supplemental questions.

key discussion questions

- What does it mean to you personally to be part of God's family?
- When someone doesn't show up for worship or Sunday school, who is let down? How can each person be more present and fully engaged?
- What would it take for you to be more involved?

supplemental questions

- Do you think that you sometimes act or think as a pauper, instead of as a prince or princess? In what

ways? What prevents you from moving from the
servants' quarters?
- Why are some people unwilling to risk rejection in
  order to help God's family grow?
- Are you willing to accept other people as God created
  them? Are you willing to allow God to determine
  when and what to change about them?

looking ahead

During the coming week, we'll read more about gifts. This
Scripture will help us meditate on what's most important:

> What can I offer the LORD
> for all he has done for me?
>
> —Psalm 116:12

part IV

pennies in the
fountain

22: Maintaining balance

insight _____

_____

_____

_____

_____

application _____

_____

_____

_____

_____

23: Heavenly treasure

insight _____

_____

_____

_____

_____

application _____

_____

_____

_____

_____

24: Keeping priorities in line

insight _____

_____

_____

_____

_____

application _____

_____

_____

_____

_____

25: Facts and figures

insight _____

_____

_____

_____

_____

application _____

_____

_____

_____

_____

26: A cheerful giver

insight _____
_____
_____
_____
_____
_____

application _____
_____
_____
_____
_____
_____

27: Faith is rewarded

insight _____
_____
_____
_____
_____
_____

application _____
_____
_____
_____
_____
_____

28: Riches beyond measure

insight _____

_____

_____

_____

_____

application _____

_____

_____

_____

_____

small group

introduction

Let's pray *(prayer)*.

This concludes our fourth week of study. Part III was about being a member of the family of God. Last week, we read about gifts and how a generous heart can make us more like Jesus. Can you recall this week's Scripture? Write it below, and then we'll all say it together.

_____

_____

_____

_____

_____

Now, let's view this week's DVD message from John Ed Mathison.

post-dvd discussion

Fill in the blanks, then dive deeper into each concept.

1. Jesus spoke about _____ more than any other topic in the Bible.
    Why do you think Jesus considered it so important?
2. Money can be a _____ that God can use to extend his Kingdom.
    What are some of the ways a church might use money for the greater good?
3. Giving offers us a chance to be more like _____.
    How can a Christian's generosity demonstrate Christ to the world?

4. A tithe is _____ percent of whatever we take in.

   What could giving a regular tithe teach us about obedience and faith?

5. Giving is not about the numbers, it's about the _____ of the giver.

   Why is the way we spend our money a picture of our priorities?

6 We can't expect a bountiful _____ if we're not willing to plant the seeds.

   How does our giving open the door for God to be increasingly generous in return?

personal application

Now, divide into smaller groups to discuss questions about the week's readings.

key discussion questions

- It's often said that it's more blessed to give than to receive. Why? Do you believe it?
- How can we focus more on God's ability to take care of us, rather than focus on our fears about adequate provision?

supplemental questions

- Have you ever asked God how much you're to give, either on a weekly basis or in a specific circumstance?
- What does giving reveal about a person's heart?
- Does the way you handle money motivate God to give you more?
- Do you believe that the more you give, the more resources God entrusts to you?

part IV

looking ahead

During the coming week, we'll read about service. This Scripture will help us stay focused.

> I, the Son of Man, came here not to be served but to serve others, and to give my life as a ransom for many.
>
> —Matthew 20:28

part V

offering a drink
to others

29: Imitate Christ

insight _____

_____

_____

_____

_____

application _____

_____

_____

_____

_____

30: A life worthwhile

insight _____

_____

_____

_____

_____

application _____

_____

_____

_____

_____

31: Opportunities abound

insight _____

_____

_____

_____

_____

_____

application _____

_____

_____

_____

_____

32: Team spirit

insight _____

_____

_____

_____

_____

application _____

_____

_____

_____

_____

33: A servant's heart

insight _____

_____

_____

_____

_____

application _____

_____

_____

_____

_____

34: Pleasing God

insight _____

_____

_____

_____

application _____

_____

_____

_____

35: Small price to pay

insight _____

_____

_____

_____

_____

application _____

_____

_____

_____

_____

small group

_____

introduction

Let's begin with prayer *(prayer)*.

We've just finished the fifth week in our study of *Treasures of the Transformed Life*. You remember that Part IV was about giving and strategically placing ourselves to receive all that God has in store for us. This past week, however, we've been focusing on service. Last week's Scripture verse fits right in. Write it below, and then we'll say it together.

_____

_____

_____

_____

_____

Let's see what John Ed Mathison has to say on this week's DVD.

post-dvd discussion

Let's begin our discussion by filling in the blanks, then diving deeper into each concept.

1. Jesus didn't have to be recruited. He simply saw a _____ and found ways to meet it.
   How can serving others allow us to be more like Jesus?
2. As a follower of Christ, serving isn't really an option; it's _____.
   Why is it so important for us to offer our time and talents?

3. The biblical standard of serving means doing the _____ we can, with what we have, where we are.

   How can God use our acts of service to teach us about faith, commitment, and dependence on him?

4. While you search for the best place to get involved, ask yourself: What am I most _____ about? What gets me the most excited?

   What's the difference in volunteering for an activity and waiting to be asked to do one?

5. When everybody enthusiastically does their part, the church can be a winning _____.

   What does it mean for the church to "win"?

6. Those who serve most effectively are not necessarily the ones who are the most talented, gifted, or trained. Instead, they're the ones who are connected to _____.

   How can God use our weaknesses to show himself to other people?

personal application

Divide into smaller groups to discuss the following questions. If you have time, also discuss some of the supplemental questions.

key discussion questions

- Discuss a time someone selflessly served you. How were you affected?
- How has serving someone else changed you? How would you like to be changed by service?

supplemental questions

- What's the best thing you ever experienced while serving?
- Serving others isn't always easy. How do you put up with the unpleasant aspects of serving?

- If someone doesn't have a lot of time to serve, what would be easy ways for that person to begin?
- What area of service within the church appeals to you the most?

looking ahead

During the coming week, we'll dive into the concept of commitment. Here's a Scripture verse on that subject to help us remember what's most important:

And now, just as you accepted Christ Jesus as your Lord, you must continue to live in obedience to him. Let your roots grow down into him and draw up nourishment from him, so you will grow in faith, strong, and vigorous in the truth you were taught. Let your lives overflow with thanksgiving for all he has done.

—Colossians 2:6–7

part VI

filling the bucket
to overflowing

36: Where you're headed

insight _____
_____
_____
_____
_____

application _____
_____
_____
_____
_____

37: Spiritual maturity

insight _____
_____
_____
_____
_____

application _____
_____
_____
_____
_____

38: Sharing your faith

insight _____

_____

_____

_____

_____

application _____

_____

_____

_____

_____

39: A standard of excellence

insight _____

_____

_____

_____

_____

application _____

_____

_____

_____

_____

40: Claim your treasure

insight _____

_____

_____

_____

_____

application _____

_____

_____

_____

_____

_____

small group

introduction

Let's pray *(prayer)*.

It's a little bit difficult to believe that we're wrapping up our study. Have you been challenged and inspired over the past six weeks?

The fifth part was about how important it is for us to reach out in service to others. This past week, we've read a lot about what happens next. The truth is, we're responsible for what we've learned so far. Our most recent Scripture reminds us to keep pressing on. Can you recall it? Write it below, and then we'll say it together.

Now let's view a final DVD message from John Ed Mathison.

post-dvd discussion

Let's open up some discussion with the following questions.

1. Regularly studying the _____ can help us know God better, and it can also help us know ourselves.

   How can God use the Bible to speak to us?

2. We risk falling back into _____ _____ before new ones are established.

   How can we make sure what we've learned in recent weeks will stick with us?

3. When we seek God with all of our hearts, it's an act of
    _____.

    How can we increase our desire for God?
4. No matter how you feel about it, the number one job of the
    church today is to _____.

    How can bringing other people into God's Kingdom
    allow us to grow in our faith, as well?
5. We don't have to be _____ to be accepted by God; he
    meets us where we are, and then helps us grow.

    How can we measure our growth in God?
6. We can be certain that God _____ us and will never
    _____ us.

    How can our confidence in him change the way we live
    our lives?

personal application

Divide into smaller groups to discuss the following questions.

key discussion questions

- What's the most important thing you've learned over
  the last forty days?
- Of the four areas of emphasis we've discussed—
  prayers, presence, gifts, and service—which one has
  meant the most to you during this time? Which one
  would you like to dive into more deeply?

supplemental questions

- Have you seen this study affect your congregation
  over the past forty days? How?
- Is there something you discovered in this study that
  you will turn to the next time you feel thirsty?

looking ahead

Since this is the final week of our study, we won't have a new Scripture verse for memorization. Instead, let's review the ones we've learned during the past weeks. We should continue to hide God's Word in our hearts, so we can go forward with confidence, wisdom, and hearts full of love, grace, and commitment.

prayer

I am the vine; you are the branches. Those who remain in me, and I in them, will produce much fruit.

—John 15:5

presence

Since we are all one body in Christ, we belong to each other, and each of us needs all the others.

—Romans 12:5

gifts

What can I offer the LORD
for all he has done for me?

—Psalm 116:12

service

I, the Son of Man, came here not to be served but to serve others, and to give my life as a ransom for many.

—Matthew 20:28

pressing on

And now, just as you accepted Christ Jesus as your Lord, you must continue to live in obedience to him. Let your roots grow down into him and draw up nourishment from him, so you will grow in faith, strong, and vigorous in the truth you were taught. Let your lives overflow with thanksgiving for all he has done.

—Colossians 2:6–7

appendix A

tips for small group leaders

Congratulations! If you've been asked to lead this Sunday school or small group study on *Treasures of the Transformed Life: Satisfying Your Soul's Thirst for More*, it means somebody sees something in you—a leadership quality, a certain spiritual maturity, or maybe even just a contagiously joyful attitude. Then again, maybe you felt it was God himself who put you up to leading the group, and you found yourself volunteering for the position before you realized what was happening.

Either way, here's good news: No matter what doubts or concerns you may have about leading this study, God will fill in the gaps. The most important thing to remember is that no matter what happens, you're not alone. He has plans for each and every person in your small group—including you—and his purposes will be accomplished.

So how can you make sure that happens? First and foremost, you have to pray. Only by staying connected to the Source can you find out what God truly wants to do. And only through prayer can you receive the encouragement and support your heart will need.

This study is about transforming lives and helping people walk more closely with God. It's unfortunate that we have a very real enemy who will try to keep that from happening. Prayer will help keep you on your guard, and will help thwart the enemy's schemes to make this a difficult study.

Pray for your ability to lead well, and remember to also pray regularly for the people in your small group. Pray that their hearts and minds would be open to whatever God has for them.

preparation

In addition to prayer, there's something else that's important: taking the time to prepare for each week's study ahead of time. That will help you feel comfortable with the subject and enable you to keep things on track during the meeting. Read through the week's chapters a couple of times, and review the answers to the fill-in-the blank questions in Appendix B. Give some thought to the associated discussion questions so you can offer suggestions if your students are not participating as much as you had expected.

Arrive a bit early to your small group meeting so you won't be rushed and harried. Check your audio/visual equipment, and make sure that everything is working properly for playing the week's DVD message.

ad hoc small groups

It's expected that many of the groups using this resource will be existing small groups or Sunday school classes. If that's the case, you can skip to the next section, Leading the Meeting.

If, however, the small group you're leading has been organized specifically for this study and isn't a regularly meeting group, you'll probably want to begin the first couple of meetings with general introductions, since it's possible that not everyone in the group will already be acquainted. Introduce yourself, and perhaps tell the group how long you've been a member of the church. Then ask the others to introduce themselves one at a time to the rest of the group. You might begin with someone you know or you might select the person nearest you. If you have several members who don't know each other, consider providing name tags for the first couple of meeting.

leading the meeting

It's always good to start the meeting with prayer. You can pray yourself or you can ask someone else to pray, if you so desire. An appropriate prayer might be something like this:

> Dear Heavenly Father, thank you for this opportunity to come together as a group and to share our thoughts, insights, and prayers regarding this forty-day study. We thank you for your presence with us now and as we go through these six weeks. We ask for your involvement and guidance for our entire congregation as we participate in this life-transforming program. We ask you to be with us and to guide our discussion today, and we ask that your will be done. We ask this in Jesus' name. Amen.

In leading this study, your main responsibility is to facilitate a flow of conversation. It's not necessary for you to have all the answers. In fact, it's probably a good thing if you don't have all the answers. Asking for input from others can help them better relate to you.

Sometimes, one or two individuals may tend to dominate the discussion. If this happens, thank them for their input, scan the room, then ask if anyone else has something they'd like to add. It's okay to encourage people by making eye contact and calling on them if they seem to have something to contribute.

While going over the discussion questions, it might help to have a poster board and a marker (or even a chalkboard) at the front of the room to write down responses. The more senses that are involved in learning something, the better your group will remember it. Enabling people to both hear and see the responses, as well as encouraging them to take notes, will help the answers stay with them.

If you don't get through all of the discussion questions before it's time to move on, that's all right—as long as the discussion is still fruitful. Remember that the Holy Spirit might take things in a slightly different direction than you had planned; do your best to remain flexible. If some questions remain, simply tell the group that it's time for discussing personal application, and encourage them to later answer the questions on their own.

When it is time to divide into smaller groups for personal application, limit each group to no more than five people, so they'll have an opportunity to share. You can determine who will be in which group in a number of ways: Group people together according to where they're sitting, separate according to men and women, allow people to choose groups for themselves, or have them pick numbers from a hat as they arrive for the meeting.

Some people will feel more comfortable sharing if they're in a group with people they don't know as well as the ones they came with; others will want to share with their friends. How you divide into smaller groups is really your choice.

Be clear at the outset about how long they're supposed to be in the smaller groups, and give a one-minute warning to wrap up when the time draws to a close.

Speaking of time, here's a general outline of how long to spend on each activity:

Timetable

Prayer	1–5 minutes
Weekly Introduction	10–15 minutes
DVD Message	8–10 minutes
Post-DVD Discussion	20 minutes
Personal Application	10–15 minutes
Looking Ahead	5–10 minutes

You probably noticed that there's a little flexibility in the number of minutes for each activity. This study was designed to work for groups that meet for approximately forty-five minutes to one hour. Feel free to adjust the time to meet your group's specific needs.

strategic scheduling

In most cases, this study will be done on Sunday mornings, the same day the pastor delivers a message on the week's topic. In some instances, however, groups may be scheduled to meet during the week, such as on Wednesday nights. If that's the case, try to schedule the weekly studies to finish the week's readings before the pastor speaks on the topic, rather than after. This gives the members of the small group a chance to cover all of the materials and have a few days to pray and further consider their responses before the topic is covered in the large assembly. It will mean a little more work during the first week to fit seven days' worth of lessons into a shorter time span, but it will be worth the effort.

setting an example

Finally, keep in mind that it's important for you to provide a positive example. Your level of enthusiasm, excitement, and commitment to the study will be contagious. As the saying goes, "The speed of the leader is the speed of the gang." As such, do your best to keep up with daily readings, prepare responses, share what you're learning, and encourage participation among your church family. You have the opportunity to help the individuals in your small group change before your very eyes—and the whole experience could be even more gratifying than you could imagine.

appendix B

Fill-in-the-Blank Answer Key

part I	part IV
unsatisfied	money
empty	tool
committed	Jesus
real	10
purpose	heart
Christians	harvest

part II	part V
distant	need
trees	essential
conversation	best
magic	passionate
partner	team
standing; gap	God

part III	part VI
family	Bible
encourage	old habits
multiply	devotion
disconnected	fish
busy	perfect
unity	loves; leave

treasures *of the* transformed life

satisfying your soul's thirst for more

Y ou'll go deeper into the *Treasures of the Transformed Life* with this companion workbook to the book of the same name by John Ed Mathison. Designed to facilitate discussion in small groups, the *Treasures of the Transformed Life Participant's Workbook* also contains personal journaling pages to record insights and applications from daily readings in the main study book. You'll get more out of the forty-day study when you use this workbook to prepare for your small group meeting or Sunday school class, and take a few quiet minutes each day to reflect on your reading.

ISBN 0-687-33455-1

ISBN 978-0-687-33455-1

9 780687 334551

90000

Abingdon Press

Cover Art: Steve Cohen/FoodPix/Jupiterimages.

Cover Design: Joey McNair